Welcome Night

Poems chosen by
Richard Brown and Kate Ruttle

Illustrated by Nick Maland

CAMBRIDGE
UNIVERSITY PRESS

Cambridge Reading

General Editors
Richard Brown and Kate Ruttle

Consultant Editor
Jean Glasberg

For Eloise

Published by the Press Syndicate of the University of Cambridge
The Pitt Building, Trumpington Street, Cambridge CB2 1RP
40 West 20th Street, New York, NY10011-4211, USA
10 Stamford Road, Oakleigh, Melbourne 3166, Australia

First published 1996

Welcome Night
This selection © Richard Brown and Kate Ruttle 1996
Illustrations © Nick Maland 1996

Printed in Great Britain at the University Press, Cambridge

A catalogue record for this book is available from the British Library

ISBN 0 521 49990 9 paperback

Acknowledgements

We are grateful to the following for permission to reproduce poems:
'Cat in the Dark' by John Agard from *I Din Do Nuttin*. The Bodley Head.
'After Dark' © Richard Brown, 1996. 'Night Street' by Richard Brown from *The Midnight Party*. Copyright © Cambridge University Press, 1993.
'Silverly' © Dennis Lee, 1983. Reproduced by permission of Westwood Creative Artists Ltd.
'Some One' by Walter de la Mare from *The Complete Poems of Walter de la Mare*, 1969 (USA: 1970). Reprinted by permission of The Literary Trustees of Walter de la Mare, and The Society of Authors as their representative.
'If You Go Softly' by Jenifer Kelly Flood from *Someone is Flying Balloons*. Omnibus, 1983.
'Dream Variations' by Langston Hughes from *Selected Poems*. Vintage Books.
'In the Mountains' by Sun Yi-Yuan from *Old Friend From Far Away*, translated by C.H. Kwock & Vincent McHugh, North Point Press, San Francisco, 1980. British English spelling is used by permission of the translators.
'Swans in the Night' by Joan Mellings from *Someone is Flying Balloons*. Omnibus, 1983.
'I Like to Stay Up' by Grace Nichols. Copyright © Grace Nichols, 1984. Reproduced with permission of Curtis Brown Group Ltd, London on behalf of Grace Nichols.
'Still Night Thoughts' by Li Po from *Chinese Lyricism,* translated by Burton Watson. Copyright © Columbia University Press. Reprinted with permission of the publisher.
'I'm Alone in the Evening' by Michael Rosen from *Mind Your Own Business*. Scholastic Publications Ltd.
'Night Comes . . .' by Beatrice Schenk de Regniers from *A Bunch of Poems and Verses* by Beatrice Schenk de Regniers. Copyright © 1977 by Beatrice Schenk de Regniers. Used by permission of Marian Reiner for the author.
'Windy Nights' and 'Bed in Summer' by R.L. Stevenson.

Every effort has been made to reach copyright holders; the publishers would like to hear from anyone whose rights they have unknowingly infringed.

Contents

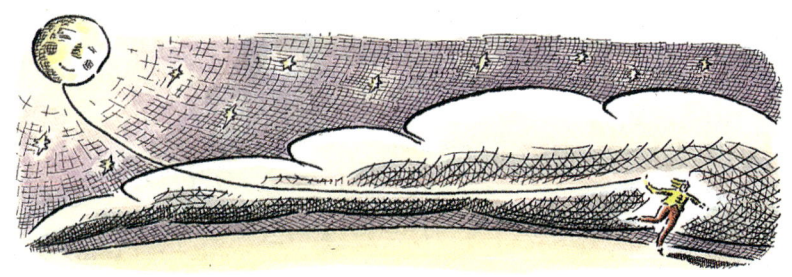

I'm Alone in the Evening   *Michael Rosen*   4
Dream Variations   *Langston Hughes*   6
Night Comes . . .   *Beatrice Schenk de Regniers*   8
The Night is a Big Black Cat   *G. Orr Clark*   9
The Ocean of the Sky   *Hitomaro*
   (translated by Arthur Waley)   10
Still Night Thoughts   *Li Po*
   (translated by Burton Watson)   11
Bed in Summer   *Robert Louis Stevenson*   12
Silverly   *Dennis Lee*   13
I Like to Stay Up   *Grace Nichols*   14
Night Street   *Richard Brown*   16
Some One   *Walter de la Mare*   20
Windy Nights   *Robert Louis Stevenson*   21
In the Mountains   *Sun Yi-Yuan*
   (translated by C.H. Kwock and Vincent McHugh)   22
Swans in the Night   *Joan Mellings*   23
If You Go Softly   *Jenifer Kelly Flood*   24
The Waves   *Australian Aboriginal (Laragia)*   26
Listen to the Tree Bear   *Peggy Appiah*   27
from **The Highwayman**   *Alfred Noyes*   28
The Lighthouse   *Enid Madoc-Jones*   29
Cat in the Dark   *John Agard*   30
After Dark   *Richard Brown*   31

Index of first lines   32

I'm Alone in the Evening

I'm alone in the evening
when the family sits
reading and sleeping
and I watch the fire in close
to see flame goblins
wriggling out of their caves
for the evening

Later I'm alone
when the bath has gone cold around me
and I have put my foot
beneath the cold tap
where it can dribble
through valleys between my toes
out across the white plain of my foot
and bibble bibble into the sea

I'm alone

when mum's switched out the light
my head against the pillow
listening to ca thump ca thump
in the middle of my ears.
It's my heart.

Michael Rosen

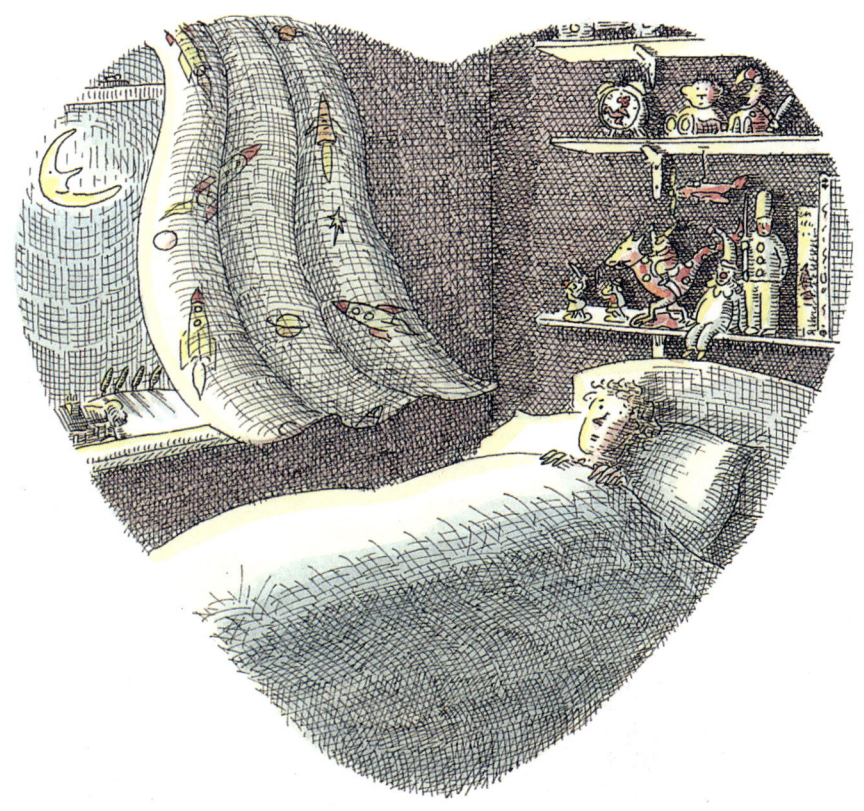

Dream Variations

To fling my arms wide,
In some place of the sun,
To whirl and to dance
Till the white day is done,
Then rest at cool evening
Beneath a tall tree
While night comes on gently,
      Dark like me, –
That is my dream!

To fling my arms wide,
In the face of the sun,
Dance! whirl! whirl!
Till the quick day is done,
Rest at pale evening . . .
A tall, slim tree . . .
Night coming tenderly,
        Black like me.

Langston Hughes

Night Comes . . .

Night comes
leaking
out of the sky.

Stars come
peeking.

Moon comes
sneaking,
silvery-sly.

Who is
shaking,
shivery-
quaking?

Who is afraid
of the night?

Not I.

Beatrice Schenk de Regniers

The Night is a Big Black Cat

The Night is a big black cat
   The Moon is her topaz eye,
The stars are the mice she hunts at night,
   In the field of the sultry sky.

G. Orr Clark

The Ocean of the Sky

In the ocean of the sky
Through a wave-rising of clouds
The ship of the moon
Seems to be rowing along
Through a forest of stars.

Hitomaro

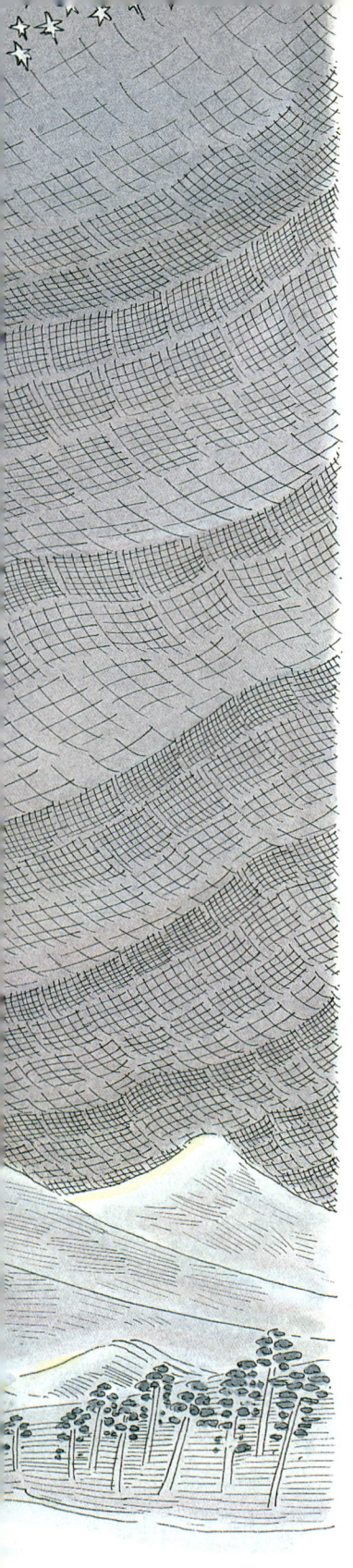

Still Night Thoughts

Moonlight in front of my bed –
I took it for frost on the ground!
I lift my eyes to watch the mountain moon,
lower them and dream of home.

Li Po

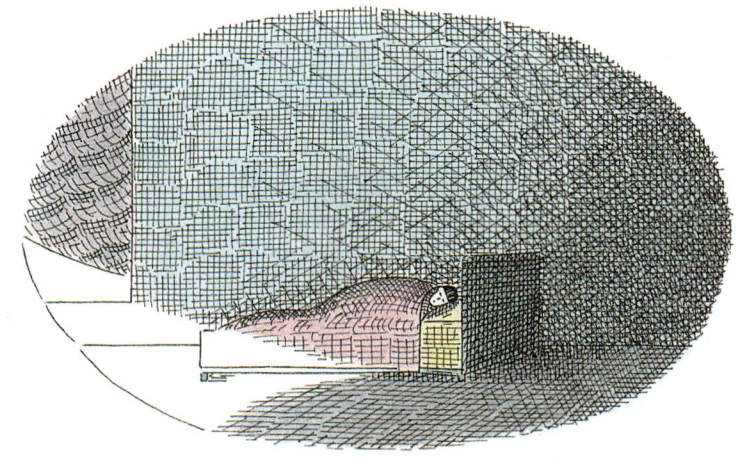

Bed in Summer

In winter I get up at night
And dress by yellow candle-light.
In summer, quite the other way,
I have to go to bed by day.

I have to go to bed and see
The birds still hopping on the tree,
Or hear the grown-up people's feet
Still going past me in the street.

And does it not seem hard to you,
When all the sky is clear and blue
And I should like so much to play,
To have to go to bed by day?

Robert Louis Stevenson

Silverly

Silverly,
  Silverly,
Over the
  Trees
The moon drifts
  By on a
Runaway
  Breeze.

Dozily,
  Dozily,
Deep in her
  Bed,
A little girl
  Dreams with the
Moon in her
  Head.

Dennis Lee

I Like to Stay Up

I like to stay up
and listen
when big people talking
jumbie stories

I does feel
so tingly and excited
inside me

But when my mother say
"Girl, time for bed"

Then is when
I does feel a dread

Then is when
I does cover up
from me feet to me head

Then is when
I does wish I didn't listen
to no stupid jumbie story

Then is when
I does wish I did read
me book instead

Grace Nichols

Jumbie is the Guyanese word for ghost.

Night Street

A poem for three voices

Half-asleep and half-awake,
who can tell what's true?
　　Footsteps in the street outside:
　　Dad, can that be you?

1　As I lay in my bed
　　with the moon on my sheet,
　　I heard the soft thud
　　of a giant's feet. Scared,
　　　　I quivered,
　　　　shook and
　　　　shivered,
　　　　huddled in the dark.
　　　　All at once –
　　　　a silence
　　　　and a lone dog's bark.

Half-asleep and half-awake,
who can tell what's true?
  Footsteps in the street outside:
   Dad, can that be you?

2   As I lay in my bed
    clasping my sheet,
    not a giant I heard,
    but a dragon's feet. Scared,
        I shivered,
        terrified,
        quivered,
        huddled in my bed.
        All at once –
        a silence
        pressing round my head.

*Half-asleep and half-awake,
who can tell what's true?
Footsteps in the street outside:
Dad, can that be you?*

3 As I lay in my bed
tight in my sheet,
I heard nothing but the patter
of goblin feet. Scared,
I shivered,
shook and
gibbered,
hiding in my bed.
All at once –
a laugh
cackled in my head.

*Half-asleep and half-awake,
who can tell what's true?
    Footsteps in the street outside:
    Dad, can that be you?*

1   At night our street's mysterious,
    full of ghostly sound . . .

2   Heavy footsteps, whisperings,
    make our hearts pound.

3   Just a silly nightmare,
    our parents like to say . . .

*Giant, dragon, goblin?
    Only light keeps them at bay.*

Richard Brown

Some One

Some one came knocking
At my wee, small door;
Some one came knocking,
I'm sure – sure – sure;
I listened, I opened,
I looked to left and right,
But nought there was a-stirring
In the still dark night;
Only the busy beetle
Tap-tapping in the wall,
Only from the forest
The screech-owl's call,
Only the cricket whistling
While the dewdrops fall,
So I know not who came knocking,
At all, at all, at all.

Walter de la Mare

Windy Nights

Whenever the moon and stars are set,
Whenever the wind is high,
All night long in the dark and wet,
A man goes riding by.
Late in the night when the fires are out,
Why does he gallop and gallop about?

Whenever the trees are crying aloud,
And ships are tossed at sea,
By, on the highway, low and loud,
By at the gallop goes he;
By at the gallop he goes, and then
By he comes back at the gallop again.

Robert Louis Stevenson

In the Mountains

Travelling back and forth
                    I meet
                  no one
my hut
        deep in the mountains
A lone crane
            starts up with a rush
            in front of me
the draught he makes
            stirring trees
            in the moonlight

Sun Yi-Yuan

Swans in the Night

Three swans
Under the moon,
Three shadows
On the lagoon.

Three swans
On the water ride,
Three shadows
Move beside.

Silver water,
Silent swans,
Swaying ferns
With silvered fronds.

A strolling cloud
Obscures the moon,
Gone the swans
From the dark lagoon.

Joan Mellings

If You Go Softly

If you go softly out to the gum trees
At night, after the darkness falls,
If you go softly and call –
   Tch, Tch, Tch,
   Tch, Tch, Tch,
   They'll come –
   the possums!

If you take bread that you've saved
They'll come close up, and stand
And eat right from your hand –
   Softly,
   Snatching,
   Nervous –
   the possums!

And if you are still, and move slowly,
You can, very softly, pat
Their thick fur, gently, like that –
   It's true!
   You can!
   Really touch them –
   the possums!

You can do that all –
If you go softly,
At night,
To the gum trees,
If you go softly
– and call.

*Jenifer
Kelly Flood*

The Waves

Waves coming up: high waves coming up against the rocks,

Breaking, shi! shi!

When the moon is high with light upon the waters:

Spring tide; tide flowing to the grass,

Breaking, shi! shi!

In its rough waters, the young girls bathe.

Hear the sound they make with their hands as they play!

Australian Aboriginal (Laragia)

Listen to the Tree Bear

Listen to the tree bear
Crying in the night
Crying for his mammy
In the pale moonlight.

What will his mammy do
When she hears him cry?
She'll tuck him in a cocoa-pod
And sing a lullaby.

Peggy Appiah

from **The Highwayman**

The wind was a torrent of darkness among the gusty trees,
The moon was a ghostly galleon tossed upon cloudy seas,
The road was a ribbon of moonlight over the purple moor,
And the highwayman came riding –
Riding – riding –
The highwayman came riding up to the old inn door.

Alfred Noyes

The Lighthouse

The sun's last light has gone,
The night has veiled the trees;
Has hid the road that winds beyond,
The roof-tops and the eaves.

There is no moon or star,
No guiding lamp to gleam,
Only the lighthouse, standing far,
Swings high one level beam.

Enid Madoc-Jones

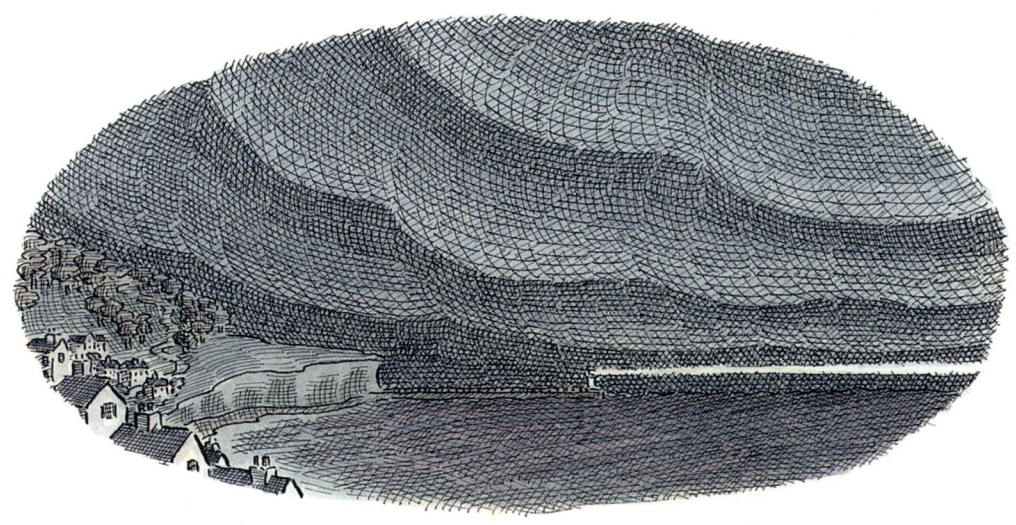

Cat in the Dark

Look at that!
Look at that!

But when you look
there's no cat.

Without a purr
just a flash of fur
and gone
like a ghost.

The most
you see
are two tiny
green traffic lights
staring at the night.

John Agard

After Dark

Strike a match
in the dark.

The brave little
flame
eats the night

and leaves
a little black
grin
in your fingers.

Richard Brown

Index of first lines

Half-asleep and half-awake   16
I like to stay up   14
If you go softly out to the gum trees   24
I'm alone in the evening   4
In the ocean of the sky   10
In winter I get up at night   12
Listen to the tree bear   27
Look at that!   30
Moonlight in front of my bed   11
Night comes   8
Silverly   13
Some one came knocking   20
Strike a match   31
The Night is a big black cat   9
The sun's last light has gone   29
The wind was a torrent of darkness among the gusty trees   28
Three swans   23
To fling my arms wide   6
Travelling back and forth   22
Waves coming up: high waves coming up against the rocks   26
Whenever the moon and stars are set   21